MY DAILY PRAYER

My Daily Prayer

 A SHORT SUPPLICATION FOR
EVERY DAY IN THE YEAR

F. B. MEYER

Fleming H. Revell Company

PRINTED IN THE UNITED STATES OF AMERICA

Library of Congress Catalog Card Number: 57-12366

Westwood, New Jersey

I.4

MY DAILY PRAYER

~~~ *January* ~~~

1. (New Year's Day.) Be with me, Lord, as I step out on the untrodden way of this new year. I know not what it may bring of joy or sorrow, of temptation or service; but I humbly commit myself and my way to Thee. Make the best that Thou canst of me for Thy glory.

2. I bless Thee, O Son of God, that there is no need for me to go up to heaven to bring Thee down, or into Thy grave to bring Thee up. Thou art here, in this hour and at this place. I confess Thee as Lord, and believe in my heart that Thou art risen from the dead.

3. Thou hast said, O Lord Jesus, that he that believeth in Thee hath everlasting life; I do now believe; with my whole heart I look to Thee as Saviour, Friend, and King; and in this glad hour I receive from Thy hand, not only life, but life more abundantly.

4. Deliver me, O my Lord and Master, from self-confidence, self-centeredness, and self-consciousness. Be Thou my confidence, and the center of my activities; and may I always be more conscious of Thy presence than of the presence or absence of others.

5. Fix my heart, O Lord, on Thyself, that amid the changes and chances of this mortal life I may be kept steadfast and unmovable and ever abounding in Thy work.

6. Lord Jesus, Who knowest the weakness of my mortal nature, take away from me the fear of death, and when I come to the last, open for me the beautiful gate of life, that I may pass through it into the Eternal Temple of God.

7. Lord, it is not in man to direct his way. I pray Thee that I may never lean unto my own understanding, but trusting in Thee with all my heart, may I be led in the way everlasting.

8. Fill me with Thy joy, O Lord, that I may have wherewith to give to my home and friends, and to the great sad world around me. Keep me from hiding my light under the bushel of my own anxieties.

9. Help me, dear Lord, to walk in the footsteps of Thy holy life; denying myself and becoming poor that those around me may be made rich. Teach me how to gain by giving, and to find by losing, according to Thy Word.

10. My heart, O my God, is broken and contrite for all the sin and failure of my life. I can only bring it to Thee as my best sacrifice; and I thank Thee for Thy promise not to despise it.

11. Make me, O blessed Master, strong in heart, full of courage, fearless of danger, holding pain and danger cheap when they lie in the path of duty. May I be strengthened with all might by Thy Spirit in the inner man.

12. Almighty God, speed Thy gospel round the world, that all nations may soon have heard its glorious message, and may Thy strayed flock come back to the one Fold—Thy heart, and to the one Shepherd—Thine only begotten Son.

13. By day and by night, in life and in death, may I ever be true to Thee, O Lover of my soul, my ceaseless Friend, my unchangeable Saviour. Into Thy hands, I commit my spirit.

14. I turn to Thee, O Merciful God! To whom else could I go? My sins are many, but Thy mercy is great; my sins are swift, but Thine anger is slow; my tears are bitter, but Thy tenderness is sweet and sure. Let Thy gentleness make me great.

15. O God my Father, to Thee nothing is small and nothing great, the ages are as sands on the shore and nations as drops in the bucket. Help me to look, not at this affliction, which is but for a moment, but to the far more exceeding and eternal weight of glory.

16. Grant me, O Lord, I pray Thee, a keen sensitiveness to all that is beautiful in nature and lovely in my fellow men, that I may see Thy beauty everywhere, and be changed into the same image.

17. Make me, O divine Friend, strong and pure in my friendship, that I may never break down barriers which I ought to maintain, or withhold that which I ought to give for the help and comfort of others.

18. Give me grace, O Thou who wast tempted in all points as we are yet without sin, to be watchful against the earliest and most insidious approaches of temptation, that I may at once hide myself under the shadow of Thy wings.

19. Open to me, O Spirit of Truth, I pray Thee, the treasures of Thy Holy Word, that my soul may be continually enriched, and that I may abound in every good word and work.

20. O Gracious Giver of all things, enable me ever to remember that whatsoever Thou hast given is a sacred trust to be held and used for others, and at last may I have the humble consciousness that I have glorified Thee on the earth and finished the work which Thou gavest me to do.

21. Teach me to love Thine own beautiful world, as Thou didst love it, to whom the mountains, flowers, and birds ministered;

speak to me through all the voices of nature; and grant me a quick sensitiveness to Thy presence beneath her pure and transparent veil.

22. Withhold me, O Holy Saviour, from all filthiness of the spirit, as well as of the flesh, that I may attain to perfect holiness in the fear of the Lord.

23. O weary not of me, most blessed Comforter, who am often weary of myself. My only hope is in Thy love, which loves to the uttermost. Gird Thyself yet once again, and wash my soiled life. Thou will not quench the smoking flax nor break the bruised reed.

24. May I never profess more than I actually experience; but may the hidden things of my heart be richer and fuller and deeper than I express to any save to Thee, O searcher of hearts.

25. Come to me, Lord, in my sore brokenness. My fair ideals are like trampled flowers, and my attempts after perfection have failed, but do Thou for me what I cannot do for myself, and perfect that which concerneth me, because Thy mercy endureth forever.

26. Deliver me, O Lord, from every false way, that I may cleave to Thee with a perfect heart, and so by Thy mercy may attain to know Thee, as also I am known of Thee, through Jesus Christ.

27. Be my ruler and guide, Gracious Father, I beseech Thee, that I may so pass through things temporal as not finally to lose the things eternal.

28. Enrich me, O Lord, by the manifold gifts of Thy Holy Spirit, that I, patiently enduring through the darkness of this world, and being filled by Thy Heavenly Grace, may become a burning and shining light until the day dawn, and the shadows flee away.

29. Help me to deny myself, and be crucified unto the world, that I may follow the Lamb whithersoever He goeth, lifting up my head with holy joy, because the day of my complete redemption draweth nigh.

30. By Thy holy inspiration, O Lord, do Thou enlighten my understanding, direct my heart and mind, keep my lips, and reveal Thyself to me in the riches of Thy grace and glory.

31. Teach me evermore, O Lord, to discern Thy will and to faithfully and diligently perform the same, that my life may be to Thy glory.

February

1. Vouchsafe, O Lord, unto me and all Thy saints, the fullness of joy from Thy presence, and the treasures of goodness which are at Thy right hand.

2. Heavenly Father! We pray that Jesus Christ may become dearer to us. May we love him as a personal Friend, and hide ourselves in the hourly consciousness of His presence. May we have no taste or desire for things which He would disapprove. Let His love constrain us not to live unto ourselves, but to Him.

3. Adjust me with Thyself, and then fulfill in me, I entreat Thee, all the good pleasures of Thy goodness, and the work of faith with power.

4. May I be enabled to drink of Thy cup and be baptised with Thy baptism, that I may be near Thee when Thou comest in Thy kingdom.

5. Celestial Vine! Pour Thy vital sap through all the arteries of my soul, that I may bear much fruit for Thy glory.

6. Most Holy God, in whose sight the heavens are not clean, spare me not until my heart is cleansed, purified, and sanctified, that I may not seem better to man than I am towards Thee.

7. Help me so to live that those specially associated with me, and directing or serving me day by day, may long to have the love and joy which they see in me.

8. My all is now surrendered to Thee, my Lord, make of me as much as possible for Thy glory.

9. I long to range my will on Thy side; O my God, keep it there; that I may hate what Thou hatest, forsake what Thou wouldst have me forsake, and do what Thou callest me to accomplish.

10. Grant unto me, most gracious Lord, singleness of heart that in every word, thought, and deed, I may put Thee first, and in all humility and earnestness seek to serve Thee, and Thee only.

11. Impart to me, Heavenly Father, I pray Thee, a self-forgetful spirit, that I may be more anxious to give than to receive, more eager to understand than to be understood, more thoughtful for others, more forgetful of myself.

12. Send me, O Lord, I humbly ask, good speed this day. Teach me when to speak and when to be silent; when to act, and when to refrain from action; and in all the details of daily life, to do Thy will on earth as it is done in heaven.

13. If this day I should get lost amid the perplexities of life and the rush of many duties, do Thou search me out, gracious Lord, and bring me back into the quiet of Thy presence.

14. Give me grace, O my Father, that I may persevere in the work to which Thou hast called me, not leaving it half done, nor giving up when the first enthusiasm has faded, and when other interests arise to attract.

15. Calm me, O God, when my spirit is feverish and hot. Place Thy cool hand upon my head; and breathe the spirit of Thy calm through my heart. May I know that around my restlessness Thou art rest.

16. Make me, O Holy Father, so quick to respond to the pruning of the silver knife of Thine internal dealings with my soul, that I may be spared from bleeding under the iron knife of external pain.

17. O Heavenly Father, unveil to me, I humbly ask, the sweet mystery and beauty of that name of Thine—Abba Father.

18. May I so yield to Thee, as Thou wrestlest with and overcomest my proud nature, that I may be enabled to prevail with God and man.

19. Oh Thou who wert meek and lowly in heart, may I be genuinely humble, with the humility which does not realize that it is humble.

20. Teach me to lose the personal in the universal, and to be as triumphant in the successes of other in which I have not share, as in mine own.

21. Fill me, I entreat Thee, with a so absorbing passion for Thy kingdom and glory, that I may be eager for Thee to be glorified, though I die unrecognized and unknown.

22. Help me to believe that all things are of Thee; and that Thou hast a plan for my life, of which each passing incident is a part.

23. May I give, not things only, but myself to others, with full measure, heaped up, and running over. May I despair of none, and look for nothing again.

24. I bring to Thee, O Lord, my desires, and pray Thee to cleanse them by the searching fires of Thy pure Spirit, that I may desire those things only and to that extent, which Thou hast chosen and prepared for me.

25. Eternal God, work in me, not only to will but to do of Thy good pleasure; and may I work out what Thou dost work in.

26. Heavenly Father! Take into Thy loving care my home, my loved ones far and near, and all members of Thy great scattered family. Let me not be anxious about tomorrow's provision or path, but trust Thee to provide and lead. Open Thine hand, and satisfy the desire of every living thing.

27. I pray Thee, O my Father, to shut me up to a simpler and more confiding faith. May I trust more than I know, and believe more than I see; and when my heart is overwhelmed within me, lead me to the Rock that is higher than I.

28. Help me, my Father, to believe that tomorrow is but one of the many mansions in Thy house, that Thou wilt be with me, and that as my day so shall my strength be.

29. Send me, gracious Lord, the Comforter; may He fill my nature as the rain fills the pools; and may the parched ground of my heart become as a garden. Instead of the thorn may there come up the fir tree and instead of the briar, the myrtle.

ᆥᅠ*March* ᆥᅠ

1. Blessed Lord! As far as it lieth in my power, may I live peaceably with all men. Teach me to commit my cause to Thee, who judgest righteously, not anxious to defend or avenge myself, but always more anxious to set an example of enduring patience than to manifest the strength of our cause.

2. Lord God Almighty! look on those to whom the world is dark; send a ray of light to gladden the lonely and sad-hearted, the forsaken and forgotten, the sinful and miserable; and teach me how to comfort them, with the comfort wherewith Thou hast comforted me.

3. O Saviour, who goeth after that which is lost until Thou findest it, teach me to minister to the needs of others. May I pitifully regard those who know Thee not, and whose life is one long outrage of Thy forbearing love. Give me something of Thy Shepherd compassion and long-suffering.

4. My Father God! Let the motto of my life henceforth be "Glory to God in the Highest," for only so can there be peace in my heart and good will towards men. May my heart be kept in unison with the angels' song.

5. Set a watch, O Lord, at the door of my lips, that I may speak nothing inconsistent with perfect truth and love.

6. Gracious God, give me to behold the rainbow of hope on the dark storm clouds that brood over my life; and may I rest confidently on that covenant, ordered in all things and sure, which was sealed by the precious blood of Christ.

7. O King of Glory and Lord of Hosts, who hast ascended in triumph to the right hand of the Father, leave me not comfortless, but send upon me the promise of the Father, even the Spirit of Truth.

8. As Jesus my Lord ascended into the heavens, so grant unto me, merciful Father, that I also in heart and mind may thither ascend, and with Him continually dwell.

9. Cause me, O God, I humbly pray, to be inflamed with heavenly desires, and may Thy love be so shed abroad in my heart that I may evermore seek the things which are above, where Christ sitteth at Thy right hand.

10. Help me, O Lord, I entreat Thee, to add to my faith, strength; and to strength, knowledge; and to knowledge, self-control; and to self-control, endurance; to endurance, godliness; and to godliness, brotherly kindness; and to brotherly kindness, love. May these be in me and abound.

11. Teach me not only to bear, but to love Thy Cross. And as I take and carry it, may I find that it is carrying me.

12. Grant me concentration of purpose, and singleness of heart, that I may do, not many things, but much. Unite my heart to fear and serve Thee.

13. Heavenly Father, have mercy on those who know Thee not; take from them all ignorance, hardness of heart, and contempt of Thy Word; and so fetch them home, blessed Lord, to Thy flock, that they may be saved, and become one flock under the Great Shepherd and Bishop of souls.

14. Almighty God, I beseech Thee to raise me from the death of sin to the life of righteousness by that same power that brought the Lord Jesus from the dead, that I may walk in newness of life, and be planted in the likeness of His resurrection.

15. Heavenly Father, I know assuredly that all things are working together for my good, but help me to wait patiently and toil diligently, though the waiting be long and the toil hard.

16. Alas, O Lord, there is nothing in me that can attract or hold Thy love. I have failed so often, and cost Thee so much. Forgive that bitter past, and make me beautiful in the beauty which Thou shalt place upon me.

17. Heavenly Father, I thank Thee for the trials and pains that are ever working for my good, and making me a partaker of Thy holiness. May I receive the abundance of Thy grace, and reign in life here and hereafter.

18. Most gracious God, quicken me by Thy Holy Spirit, I pray Thee, that I may run in the way Thou hast marked out for me, with enlarged desire. Grant me the girded loin and the alert foot; and may I be ever kept looking off unto Jesus.

19. Holy Father, I thank Thee for Thy forgiving, pitying love. I gratefully realize that our sin cannot alter Thy love, though it may dim our enjoyment of it. But I entreat Thee to set me free from the love and power of sin, that it may not intercept the light of Thy countenance.

20. O Saviour, may I be permitted not only to touch the hem of Thy garment, but to lean back on Thy heart. May I be one whom Thou lovest.

21. Heavenly Father, make me like Him who, though He was rich, yet for our sakes became poor, that many, through His poverty, might be made rich. Help me to deny myself, so as to give joy and comfort to those less favored than I am; and may I learn how much more blessed it is to give than to receive.

22. Amid the temptations of the evil one, and the provocation of the ungodly, help me to abide steadfast and immovable, so as to be accounted worthy to stand before the Son of Man.

23. May the Holy Spirit bring all things to my remembrance, whenever in the heat of passion or the stress of life I am tempted to forget.

24. When temptation is near may I meet it as a soldier who is conscious that the captain is fighting at his side.

25. Withdraw my soul, I pray Thee, from the absorbing delights of this world, with its petty aims and ideals, and open mine eyes to the high joys of my inheritance in Christ.

26. Holy Spirit, teach me to put away anger, wrath, malice and evil communications, loveless words and loveless acts, and may I put on, as Thine elect, a heart of compassion, kindness, humility, meekness, long-suffering. May I forbear with and forgive others as Thou dost bear with and forgive me.

27. Hasten the coming of Thy kingdom, O Lord, the fulfillment of Thy promise, and the consummation of Thy purpose, that the travail of this world may soon usher in the rest of Thine eternal Sabbath.

28. Lord Jesus, teach me to see the soul of good in things evil; to discern the silver edge of lowering clouds; and to believe in Thy love, which is conducting me safely and by a right way to my home.

29. Heavenly Father! Thou killest and makest alive; Thou bringest down to the grave, and bringest up; Thou raisest up the poor from the dust, and liftest the needy from despair, to make them sit in heavenly places, and inherit the Throne of Glory. Glory be to Thee, O Thou most high!

30. Lord Jesus! As Thou didst love Jerusalem, teach me to love my fatherland. I pray for our ruler and the rulers of other lands; for statesmen, judges, magistrates, and all in authority; that we may be quietly and godly governed, and that peace and happiness, truth and justice, religion and piety may be established amongst us for all generations.

31. I would not hide or cloak my sins before Thy face, Almighty God, my Heavenly Father; but confess them, with a humble, lowly, penitent and obedient heart, to the end that I may receive forgiveness of the same, through Thine infinite goodness and mercy.

April

1. Most blessed Lord! Have mercy upon those who have rejected the invitation of Thy gospel, and to whom it has become a savor of death unto death. Succor those who have missed their religious privileges through sickness; or on account of bereavement; or by reason of some other cause known to Thee.

2. Most gracious God, I thank Thee for the gift of the Holy Spirit, the Comforter, pure as dew, cleansing as fire, tender and refreshing as the breath of spring. O blessed Trinity, ever engaged in giving Thy choice things to us, Thine unworthy children, accept my gratitude for which I have no words.

3. May my heart be so childlike and pure that I may see the beauty of the world around me, as it appears to the eyes of unfallen beings, and as it appeared to Thee, my Lord, when Thou didst notice the lilies and birds.

4. May I not only find forgiveness in Thy Cross, my blessed Lord, but may it produce in me rivers of living water, as the rod of Moses drew them from the rock.

5. Heavenly Father! Help me to remember that what Thou hast given Thou wilt also require; and enable me so to live that I may multiply the talents with which Thou hast entrusted me, by using them for Thy glory, and for the comfort and help of others.

6. My Saviour, may I unlade Thy ships as they come, richly freighted, for my need. May I rejoice in all the good Thou sendest, and be receptive of all things that pertain to life and godliness, that my character may abound in gold, silver, and precious stones.

7. Oh, to be wholly Thine! To have no thought closed from Thy Spirit; no act other than Thou wouldst approve; no word inconsistent with Thy perfect love; no purpose in which Thou canst not have a part.

8. May I not be satisfied with talking or musing on Thy love. Grant me the grace of manifesting it, not only in great crises, but amid petty annoyances and the daily fret.

9. Help me to meditate more intently on Thy humility and patience, O my Saviour, so that almost unconsciously these traits may reappear in my own character.

10. Holy Father! In Thee everything is found that can make Thy children glad, and I praise Thee with my whole being. Thou hast kept me whilst I slept, I have awakened in safety, and to Thee I would consecrate my renewed powers. Let the outgoings of my heart rejoice this morning.

11. I pray Thee, O Lord, to give me a ready sympathy with others, that I may look at things from their standpoint and see myself as they see me.

12. Show me, today, O Lord, that one of Thy little ones to whom I am to give a cup of cold water in Thy name.

13. Let me not dwell on the past, my Father, as though it held the best. May I dare to believe that the best is yet to be, and that Thou art filling my life with the rain of tears, every one of which will one day yield the wine of joy.

14. Lord Jesus, we thank Thee that a new day affords another opportunity for consecration and devotion. Thou hast turned a fresh page in our life's story. It comes from Thee without blemish or soil; help us to keep it so. Forgive the past blotted with our failures and sins; and help us to walk in the light.

15. Make me, O Lord, to know the hope of Thy calling, the riches of the glory of Thine inheritance in the saints, and the exceeding greatness of Thy power towards them that believe. Above all, grant me the spirit of wisdom and revelation in the knowledge of Thyself.

16. Help me, O Lord, to appreciate the sensitiveness of Thy love. May I not disappoint Thee by using exaggerated outward expressions of that which is slowly growing in the personal relations between us.

17. Lord, I cannot hope to sit on Thy right or Thy left in Thy kingdom, nor to lean on Thy bosom, but at least permit me to sit at Thy feet and hear Thy Word.

18. Father, we know that Thou dost suffer in the suffering of men, and that Thy sympathy is quick and tender and deep. We thank Thee that our blessed Lord has wept human tears, and borne the weight of human sorrow. May we comfort others with the comfort wherewith we have ourselves been comforted of God.

19. Make Thyself so real to me that my first thought in everything shall be to do Thy will, and to avoid whatever might give Thee sorrow.

20. Let me not be satisfied with refraining from sin; but as I abide in Thee, may I bear the fruits of the Spirit, which are love, joy and peace.

21. May I be quick to discern, in each person I meet, how I can help Thee in liberating that soul still further from the grave of sin, and lifting it to a life of righteousness.

22. Heavenly Father! Forgive us our many sins, ignorances, and failures, and cleanse us from all iniquity for the sake of Jesus Christ, our Lord. Accept us graciously, and love us freely. May we hate sin as Thou dost, and may Thy grace sink deeper into our hearts, purifying the springs of thought and action.

23. Teach me, my Saviour, to understand the meaning of Thy Cross, that through death with Thee there to every sin, I may enter with Thee into the fullness of life.

24. Most gracious God! Wherever at this hour there is sore sickness in home or hospital; wherever souls are passing from time into eternity; wherever there are anguish, peril and alarm, there may Thy gentle Holy Spirit instill peace and help. I ask it in the name of Jesus Christ.

25. Most blessed Lord! Hear me for those I love, especially for such as are passing through the valley of the shadow, and to whom the day brings no alleviation of pain or sorrow. Put gladness into their hearts; may light arise in their darkness; and let the days of their mourning be ended.

26. O send out Thy light and Thy truth, and let them lead me and bring me at last to my Father's house in peace.

27. Make me a bright Christian, I entreat Thee, not morbid and austere and silent, not foolish and frivolous, but radiant, glad and happy.

28. Holy Father! Give me grace to lay aside the works of darkness, and to put on the armor of light. May all self-indulgence, all that is earthly, selfish, and unholy, be put away, and may I not fail Thee in the day of battle!

29. Give me, my Father, a loving and thankful heart. May Thy mercies, like cords, bind me to the horns of Thine altar. Let nothing be held back from Thee; but may my entire nature be surrendered to Thine indwelling and service, as a palace, every room of which is freely open to its Lord.

30. O Heavenly Father, who art leading me home, help me to consider the interests of others, and to act nobly and generously towards them, because we are all Thy children, and Thine infinite resources are at our command. Make me a blessing to those I come in contact with, that I may leave upon their faces and lives some traces of that uncreated light that I have caught from the face of Christ.

~~~ *May* ~~~

1. I pray Thee, O Lord, to deliver me from the fear of death; and when mine eyes open in the dawn of heaven, may I see Thee standing to welcome me, and may I receive Thy "well done."

2. Keep me through this day from all that would grieve Thy Holy Spirit. Help me to look, not on the dark cloud, but on Thy rainbow; not on the stormy waters, but on the face of Jesus; not on what Thou hast taken or withheld, but on what Thou hast left; not on my own fickle and changeful heart, b on Thy love, which is steadfast as the great mountains.

3. For all Thy bounties, Heavenly Father, known to me, and for all unknown, accept my hearty thanks. May I not murmur at Thy Providence, or dread the unknown future. Whatever befalls me, help me to believe in Thine unfailing care, and to know that in the valley of the shadow Thou art by my side.

4. Help me never to break Thy confidence, my God, or to complain to others that Thy discipline is too severe.

5. May I anoint my head and wash my face that I may not appear unto men to suffer, but only to Thee, who seest in secret, and wilt reward me openly.

6. Keep me from running hither and thither for human sympathy. May I be satisfied with Thine. Whom have I in heaven but Thee; and on earth none is to be desired beside Thee.

7. I beseech Thee, O Lord, to give to me Thy Holy Spirit in greater measure, that His saving presence may cleanse my conscience, and His holy inspiration enlighten my heart.

8. Take from my heart, Heavenly Father, I entreat Thee, all hatred and malice, all envy and jealousy, and everything which would cause a breach between me and others; that nothing may prevent the inflowing of Thy love to my heart, and its outflowing towards others.

9. Since it is Thy will, my God, that I should suffer, give me patience, gentleness, and forgetfulness of myself, that help me to minister joy and blessing to others.

10. Give me grace, Heavenly Father, properly to administer for the benefit of others those gifts with which I am entrusted, that I may be a good steward of Thy manifold mercies, and not be ashamed before Thee at Thy coming.

11. Let me not hesitate to come to Thee, even when some shameful fall is fresh. May I dare to believe in Thine immediate forgiveness, and my restoration to the old standing in Thy dear presence.

12. Ah, Lord, my love is like some feebly-glimmering spark; I would that it were as a hot flame. Kindle it by Thy breath, till Thy love constraineth me!

13. I pray Thee, gracious Lord, that I may not miss any of those lessons which Thou art desirous of teaching me by Thy Spirit, Thy Word, and Thy Providence.

14. Help me, O Lord, to believe that what seem to be my losses are really gains, and that each ounce of affliction is adding to the weight of glory, not hereafter only, but now.

15. Keep me, Heavenly Father, as the apple of Thine eye; defend me by Thine almighty power; hide me secretly in Thy pavilion from the strife of tongues and the fiery darts of the wicked one; and may the Holy Spirit so fill me with Christ my Lord that there may be no room for anything inconsistent with love.

16. May I not be so absorbed in my own concerns as to be indifferent to the innocent joys of children and others of my home circle.

17. Lord! I pray Thee teach me to follow where Thou goest, to sit at Thy feet; and to be as true to Thee when I cannot see Thy face as in the glorious noon.

18. I ask Thee, gracious Lord, to be kept watchful and alert; so that at any moment I may discern the movement of Thy hand, and detect Thy will and guidance in the providence of little things.

19. Let me turn to Thee, O Lord, from the sweetest of earthly joys, to find that Thou art best of all, the fairest among ten thousand, and the altogether lovely.

20. I draw near to Thee, almighty and ever-living God, in the name of Thy Son Jesus Christ, my High Priest and Mediator, who hath passed into the heavens, where He ever liveth to make intercession for sinners. Forgive and accept me for His sake.

21. Turn again my captivity, O Lord, as the streams in the south. Heal my backslidings, and take not Thy Holy Spirit from me.

22. O Lord Jesus Christ, grant me such communion with Thyself that my soul may continually be athirst for that time when I shall behold Thee in Thy glory. In the meanwhile, may I behold Thy glory in the mirror of Thy Word, and be changed into the same image.

23. Help me, O Lord, daily to mortify all worldly and corrupt affections and desires, that out of my death unto sin there may arise life unto righteousness, by the grace of Thy quickening Spirit.

24. Teach me to be content to do Thy will, not looking this way or that, to compare myself with others, to seek their commendation or escape their censure. Be Thy voice my only law, Thy smile my only reward.

25. My soul awaketh early from the night, and turns to Thee, O God, for the light; for Thy light is better than life; therefore my lips shall praise Thee. Take my hand in Thine, and make the crooked places straight and the rough places plain, that Thy name may be glorified in my daily walk and conversation.

26. Grant unto me, O Lord, the blessedness of the man whom Thou choosest, and causest to approach unto Thee.

27. O my God, my heart is overwhelmed within me; lead me to the Rock that is higher than I. In the shadow of Thy wings will I make my refuge until these calamities be overpassed.

28. Thou art light, and in Thee is no darkness at all. I thank Thee for eyes to see, a heart to love, and a nature to enjoy Thy good and perfect gifts. I worship Thee, O Father of Lights, in whom is no variableness, neither shadow of turning. Enlighten my darkness, I pray Thee!

29. Lift me up, by Thy strong arm, above the mists and darkness of the valley, to stand and walk with Thee on the high level of Thy manifested presence and glory.

30. O Thou, who lovest to the end, gird Thyself, I humbly pray, and cleanse my feet, my hands, and lips from all defilement of flesh and spirit. Teach me how to perfect holiness in the fear of the Lord.

31. O my Saviour, I am overtired and weary; the strain of my life has exhausted me; the pressure of daily business has robbed me of my old elasticity and spring. I have no strength even to cast my load. Forgive me for my lack of simple, child-like faith. Come near and rest me. Take the burden I cannot cast; hush the fears I cannot allay; wipe the tears I cannot keep back.

~~~~ *June* ~~~~

1. May I not faint under Thy loving discipline, my Father, but accept it humbly and trustfully, so as to become a partaker of Thy holiness.

2. I humbly ask that I may be so filled throughout this day with thoughts of Thee, that this earthly life may be inspired with the spirit of heaven, and that I may go to and fro about my business as one who has seen the face of God, and come down to earth illuminated with the Light of Life.

3. May Thy companionship be so real to me, my Lord, that I may never feel lonely.

4. My one desire and prayer is that I may be filled with Thy love. I am bankrupt of love; I have not love enough of my own to love my neighbor as myself, and better. Shed abroad Thy love in my heart by the inspiration of Thy Holy Spirit.

5. Merciful Saviour, help me to pray for Thy one family scattered in all lands, especially for those who are united to me by the tenderest bonds of nature or of love. Encompass them with Thy tender care. Keep them from harm and sin, and from too great sorrow amid the discipline of their lives.

6. I open my nature to let in Thy blessed fullness, O Lord, and, since my capacity is small, I pray that it may be enlarged, that I may miss nothing that is possible. By love and faith, by patience and suffering, enlarge my heart, that it may be filled with all the fullness of God.

7. O Holy Spirit! Give me to know the joy that is unspeakable, the love that passeth knowledge, and the peace that passeth understanding.

8. Thou knowest my great need. Graciously draw near to me, and cover my head in the day of battle, that those evils which the craft and subtlety of the devil or man worketh against me may be brought to naught, and by the providence of Thy goodness may be dispersed.

9. Almighty God! Thou knowest that I have no power of myself to keep myself. Keep me outwardly in my body, and inwardly in my soul, that I may be defended from all adversities which may happen to the body, and from all evil thoughts which may assault and hurt the soul.

10. Teach me to pray, O Lord, as Thou didst teach Thy disciples of old, and winnow my prayers that I may desire and ask only those things which are according to Thy will.

11. Remember me, O Lord, now that Thou hast come into Thy kingdom. Keep me true to Thee through this mortal life, and present me finally, faultless, before the presence of Thy glory with exceeding joy.

12. Thou art my God, and I will praise Thee; Thou art my God, I will exalt Thee; I will give thanks unto Thee, for Thou art Love, and Thy mercy endureth forever. Constrained by Thy mercies, I present myself to Thee a living sacrifice, holy and acceptable, which is my reasonable service.

13. May I not think too little of myself, or too much, but soberly and rightly; and may I be and give to the world whatever Thou didst purpose when Thou didst send me forth.

14. I am not mine own, but Thine, O my Master, by Thy creation, Thy providence, and Thy blood; bore my ear to the door of Thy service that I may never go out from serving Thee.

15. O Holy Father! Make me humble and unselfish. Give me a childlike faith to receive what Thou dost offer, and to bear what Thou dost ordain; and may a new sense of Thy presence and power, through the Holy Spirit, abide with me.

16. O Thou true and living Vine, make me fruitful today in every good work to do Thy will. Thou hast given yearnings after a holy life; accomplish them by the grace of Thy Spirit dwelling within me and working through me continually.

17. Give unto me the pilgrim spirit; I must be in the world, may I not be of it. Give me grace to abstain from fleshly lusts, which war against the soul. May I ever obey the heavenly calling.

18. May I never forget, O Lord, that the best and happiest life must be lived in communion with the needs, sorrows, and trials of others. Give me closer sympathy with Thyself, who didst not please Thyself, but whose blessed life was perpetually laid down for others.

19. Beset me behind from the pursuit of my sins, and before from the assault of my foes, and lay Thine hand upon me to cover my head in the day of battle.

20. Deliver me, I pray Thee, Abba Father, from the fear of man, that bringeth a snare. May I fear Thee alone, with the fear born of love.

21. My heart is weary, O God. The strain of life, the cruel hatred of the world, and the failure of human love have left me desolate. I fall at Thy feet; be not silent unto me, lest I be like unto them that go down into the pit.

22. Dispose my way, Heavenly Father, and fence me round with Thy protecting care, that among all the changes and chances of this mortal life, I may ever be defended by Thy most gracious and ready help, through Jesus Christ my Lord.

23. Thou knowest, Lord, how often I am sorely let and hindered in running the race which is set before me. May Thy bountiful grace and mercy come to my help, that I may finish my course with joy, and receive the crown of life.

24. O blessed Lord, be the physician of my soul. Forgive its sins and heal its diseases. Lighten my heart in the knowledge of Thy truth, and grant me grace to pass through the remainder of this day, and of my whole life, to Thy glory.

25. Purify my heart, O God, by the fire of Thy Holy Spirit, that I may henceforth please Thee with a pure mind and serve Thee with a chaste body.

26. O most Heavenly Father, send Thy Holy Spirit, and pour into my heart that most excellent gift of love, the bond of peace and of all holiness, that I may love Thee with all my heart and soul and mind and strength, and my neighbor as myself.

27. Sprinkle my heart, O Heavenly Priest, from an evil conscience, and cleanse my life as with pure water, that I may have boldness to enter within the veil and commune with God.

28. Spirit of Truth, help me to live with an unshuttered and uncurtained heart, of which the windows are ever open to the Holy City.

29. Thou art stirring up my nest, my Father; the old is changing and giving place to the new. Spread Thy wings beneath me and teach me to trust where I can see no earthly support to rest on.

30. Thou knowest, my Saviour, how I wait for footsteps that do not come; yearn for sympathy which is withheld; knock at doors that do not open; and dread what tomorrow may bring. I shrink from the loneliness of life, and the mystery of that unknown future that stretches away in the dark like a moor beyond the light of home. But nothing can separate me from Thee.

~~~~ *July* ~~~~

1. The mountain peaks of such a life as I fain would live call to me, yet they seem too steep and high for me to reach. But Thou knowest, O Lord, and Thou hast an infinite compassion for my weakness. Fulfill in me the good pleasure of Thy will, and realize the ideals Thou hast taught me to cherish.

2. Help me, O merciful High Priest, to pray for those who have met with accident and sudden sorrow; for those who are passing through the fires, that they may not be burned; for those who are wading in deep waters, that they may not be swept down; for those who are in the midst of their foes, that they may not be overpowered; for those who are lonely, and desolate, and forlorn, that they may not lose heart.

3. O Thou who art the brightness of Thy Father's glory, and the express image of His person, may I catch some of that brightness and manifest some of that image, that men may turn from the reflection to Thee, the Eternal Reality.

4. Help me that I may not faint under Thy chastenings or be discouraged by Thy rebukes, so that at last I may partake of Thy holiness.

5. O Christ, who makest the outgoings of morning and evening to rejoice, shed on my soul Thy light, and love, and life, that my being may be as pure and radiant as Alpine heights at dawn, and noon, and eve.

6. Thou, O Christ, art all I want. May Thy grace abound towards me, so that having all sufficiency in all things, I may abound with every good work.

7. Assist me, Heavenly Father, with Thy grace, that my life may fulfill its possibilities, and that I may be enabled to walk in all such good works as Thou hast prepared for me.

8. Feed me, O Lord, with Thy flesh and blood, according to Thy promise, for they are meat and drink indeed, so that Thou mayst live in me and I in Thee, in close and ever closer union.

9. O true Vine of God, I desire to abide in Thee, that the sap of Thy life, passing through my life, may bear abundant fruit for Thy glory.

10. Heavenly Father! Send forth the tidings of Thy salvation to the ends of the earth. Be with Thy missionary servants, who are engaged in preaching the gospel to mankind. Turn the hearts of all men towards Christ, and make them obedient to the faith.

11. Heavenly Father! Hasten the time when all creation shall be delivered from the bondage of corruption to the glorious liberty of Thy children, and may Thy purpose be speedily accomplished in Thy Church, and in the coming of our Lord Jesus Christ.

12. Of Thine infinite mercy, O Lord, deliver me from the terror by night and the arrow that flieth by day, from the pestilence that walketh in darkness and from the destruction that wasteth at noonday; that leaning on Thine aid, comforted by Thy grace, and guarded by Thine angels, I may dwell in peace and safety.

13. Gracious Father! I yield to Thee my will and desires, my members and faculties, the life of my body, the thoughts of my heart, and the aspirations of my spirit—perfect, I pray Thee, that which concerneth me.

14. May I behold Thy glory, O my God, till my face and life begin to reflect it, though I wist it not.

15. O Fountain of Life, spring Thou up within me! O Light of Life, illumine me! O Source and Sun of Love, shed abroad Thy love in my heart by the Holy Ghost given unto me! O Lamb of God, who art in the midst of the throne, but who treadest the rough pathway of this world, be my Shepherd.

16. O my Father, I know that Thou lovest me, and that Thy love has chosen my path. I would have it so. Help me to be satisfied with Thy wise choice of rough and smooth, of time and tide, of sun and shower. May I finish my course with joy.

17. Teach me to do Thy will, for Thou art my God, and if I begin by choosing it, may I end by delighting in and loving it.

18. Heavenly Father, I have been a wayward child, loving my own way, and fretting too often against Thine appointment. Forgive me, I pray Thee; put away my sin; and make me as a weaned babe.

19. Grant unto me, O Heavenly Father, such faith in Thy fatherly love and mercy, that I may never be careful and troubled about the things of this life, but seek the coming of Thy kingdom and the glory of our Lord.

20. In Thy love, my Saviour, there are many mansions! Let not my heart be troubled, neither let it be afraid. Give me the Comforter and the peace that none can take away.

21. Bring near the day of Thy power, O God, and hasten the coming of Thy kingdom, that the mystery of iniquity may be brought to an end, and all men confess Jesus Christ as Lord.

22. Have mercy, I beseech Thee, on all who profess and call themselves Christians; lead them out of all their wanderings and divisions that men may see their unity in Jesus Christ, and believe that Thou didst send Him to be the Redeemer of the world.

23. Dear Lord, I am poor and weak! I have nothing worth my giving, or Thy receiving. My best was given by Thee—my holiest is defiled by sin. Take my bankrupt soul into eternal partnership with Thee, and say to me, "All that I have is thine."

24. Help me, O Lord, to take up my cross and follow Thee in the path of Thy humiliation and faith, so that I may at length behold Thy face in righteousness and receive from Thee that crown which fadeth not away.

25. O Lord Jesus Christ, Thou Captain of Salvation, who discernest the malevolence and workings of evil spirits against my soul, deliver me, I entreat Thee, amid the manifold temptations and trials by which I am beset, and make a way for me to escape; succor me by Thy mighty power, and cause me to become more than a conqueror.

26. May I love Thee, my God and Father, not for what Thou givest, but for Thyself, with a holy, absorbing and increasing love.

27. I thank Thee, O God, that Thy Blessed Son was manifested that He might destroy the works of the devil, and bring us into unity with Thyself. Deliver me, I pray Thee, from evil, and purify me even as Christ is pure.

28. Grant me grace, Heavenly Father, ever to abide steadfast in Thy faith and fear, that at last I may be accounted worthy to stand before the Son of Man.

29. Most merciful Father! I claim from Thee the fulfillment of Thy covenant promise, that Thou shouldst write Thy law upon my heart, and remember my sins and iniquities no more. May I hear Thee say, "Go, and sin no more; thy faith hath saved thee."

30. Pour down upon me, O God, the abundance of Thy mercy, forgiving those things whereof my conscience is afraid, and giving me those good things which I am not worthy to ask, through the merits and mediation of Jesus Christ, my Lord.

31. Keep me from fashioning Thee for myself, God my Saviour, after my own imaginings. May I not make a graven image of Thee, but know Thee as Thou art.

~~~~~ *August* ~~~~~

1. O King of Love, let the leaves of the Tree of Life be for my healing, and let Thy peace settle down, like the evening calm, upon my harassed nature. Minister nourishment to the fainting, and comfort to those who have failed; temper the gladness of success with the humility which attributes all glory and honor to Thy sufficient grace.

2. Lord God Almighty, how shall I ever sufficiently thank Thee for adopting me into Thy family, and making me one of Thy children? Thou hast taught me to know Thee, pray to Thee, and love Thee. Thou art my shield and my exceeding great reward. Bless me, and fill me evermore with the Spirit of Thy Son.

3. O let the great cloud of witnesses, who have gone before and entered into their rest, be to me for an example of a godly life, and even now may I be refreshed with their joy and run with patience the remainder of the race that is set before me.

4. I pray, O Heavenly Father, for those who are wandering from Thy ways in darkness and error. Have mercy upon them and convert them to Thyself. Rekindle in them the flame of Thy pure love, and restore them to their former joy, that they may praise Thee for Thy recovering mercy.

5. O Thou who knowest the wants and pitiest the infirmities of Thy people, supply unto us, out of Thine inexhaustible fullness, all those things whereof we stand in need.

6. O blessed Christ, let not sin have dominion over me. If temptation assails, may it find no foothold in my heart; if I have to pass through scenes where the infection of sin is strong, may I not be susceptible to it; if I am strongly provoked, may I not yield.

7. Prosper, I pray Thee, every great enterprise which seeks to promote peace, purity, sobriety, justice between man and man; but think on me for good, as I do lowly and obscure things with a pure desire to please Thee.

8. Be Thou, O Lord, the Alpha and the Omega of every year, month, day, hour, and act of my life. Let all things be begun, continued, and ended in Thee.

9. Let the fire of Thy love consume in me all sinful desires of the flesh and of the mind, that I may henceforth continually abide in Jesus Christ my Lord, and seek the things where He sits at Thy right hand.

10. Of Thine infinite mercy, Heavenly Father, give me such assurance of Thy protection amid the troubles and tumults of this mortal life that I may be preserved in quietness of spirit and in inward peace, ever trusting in Thy defense.

11. Grant unto me, O my Father, that I may abide faithful and steadfast, fulfilling the work of faith and labor of love which Thou hast committed to my care, that I may be well pleasing unto Thee, through Jesus Christ my Lord.

12. Thou hast given me gladness, Lord. Help me to make others glad and pass on to them the comfort wherewith Thou hast comforted me. At whatever cost, may I have fellowship with Thee in Thy redemptive purpose and ministry.

13. O Lord Jesus, show me each day how I may help Thee in opening blind eyes, and turning men from darkness to light, and from the power of Satan unto God. May Thy kingdom come; Thy power work through my hands; Thy love throb in my heart.

14. Grant unto me grace, O Lord, that I may both perceive and know what things I ought to do, and may also have grace and power faithfully to fulfill the same.

15. Comforter of the comfortless, bind my soul with Thine in intercession! Wherever there are broken hearts, bind them; captives, release them; smoking flax, fan its spark; bruised reeds, make them pillars in Thy temple. Bless especially my loved ones, and those who misunderstand and hate me. Visit them with Thy salvation, and suit Thy gifts to their several needs.

16. Let me not be put to shame, O my Lord, but make me to love and fear Thee with all my heart, that I may at last meet Thee with holy confidence and joy.

17. O true and only Shepherd, grant me grace, I pray Thee, that I may never grieve Thy Holy Spirit, or wander from the ways of Thy flock.

18. Fulfill in me, O God, those desires of goodness which Thou hast created in my heart, and perfect the work of faith, that Jesus Christ may be glorified in me, and I in Him.

19. Have mercy upon me, most merciful Father, and for the sake of Jesus Christ forgive my sins and take away all iniquity, that I may serve Thee henceforth in newness of life, to the glory of Thy holy name.

20. I thank Thee Heavenly Father, that I know Thee in Jesus Christ our Lord. He is the brightness of Thy glory, the express image of Thy person. In His face I see Thy face. I humbly ask that the Holy Spirit may open my eyes more fully to behold, and my heart more ardently to love Thee in Him.

21. O Thou Lover of All, I earnestly pray for a blessing to rest on the inmates of hospitals and workhouses; on those who have suffered long and incurably; on those who have the charge of young children; and on all whose lot is thrown in distant places, where the light of Thy gospel never shines.

22. Make me very sensitive to perceive Thee, my Lord and Master, to hear Thy voice, and to receive those gracious inspirations which come from Thine heart. May the Holy Spirit glorify Thee, taking of things that are Thine, and revealing them to me.

23. O Lord, who dost not despair of the most ignorant and unworthy, heal and save and teach me.

24. O Captain and Leader of the Holy War, may I have truth as the girdle of my loins, righteousness on my breastplate, salvation as my helmet, peace for my feet, and faith for my shield. May I have no fellowship with the unfruitful works of darkness, but reprove them by my consistent life and faithful words.

25. May my heart be as the palace, which the Stronger than the strong man keeps in perfect peace. But whatever grace may be won, or lesson learned, or sympathy gained through the fiery ordeal of temptation, let me not miss.

26. Thou art the door, O Lord! Through Thee may I pass out to my daily work and back again to rest; and whether in work or rest, may I abide in Thy safekeeping.

27. For food and raiment; for health and mental power; for friends and human love; for the beauty of nature; for the ladder between each lowly life and heaven; for the right to pray, for the open Bible; for the Rock that follows, I bless Thee, O God, and magnify Thy name.

28. We pray for this feverish, tired world; for those who know Thee not; for little children; for all who suffer and watch; for the absent, the lonely, the tired, the wayward, the sinful; for Thy servants who are on the point of fainting in their service to mankind. Succor them, O Father.

29. When the storms are high, Lord Jesus, may I feel Thee near; as when Thou camest through the mist and across the storm-swept waves, saying, "It is I; be not afraid."

30. O my Refuge, outside Thee the waves are high and the winds fierce, but in Thee I have haven, protection, peace, and blessedness. Thou art my pavilion, my refuge, my strong tower; the house of my defense, my shield and exceeding great reward. In Thee I make my refuge.

31. Lord, I thank Thee for the pillar of cloud by day and of fire by night. May I never go in front or loiter behind. When it moves in the path of duty or suffering, help me to follow; when it stays, teach me to take and use gladly the rest which Thou givest.

~~~~~ September ~~~~~

1. O my Saviour, may I live in the spirit of prayer today. There is a life of which I sometimes get a glimpse, in which the heart goes out to Thee the whole day long, smiling to Thee in joy, confiding to Thee in sorrow, and talking with Thee of all the details of daily life. Graciously make such a life mine.

2. Thy Church, O Lord, languishes for want of times of refreshing. We are poor and needy and seek water, our tongue fails for thirst. Open rivers in the high places, and fountains in the midst of the valley, make the wilderness a pool, and the dry land watersprings.

3. O Thou who hast the Key of David, who openeth and no man shutteth, who shuttest and no man openeth; go before me today, I pray Thee, opening shut gates that I may pass through them to fulfill Thy purpose in my life.

4. Heavenly Father, engraft Thy Son, Jesus Christ my Lord, inwardly in my heart, that I may bring forth the fruit of holy living, to the honor and praise of Thy name.

5. O Lord, who lovest with an everlasting love, cause Thy light and life and love to shine into my heart, that my being may be transfigured, and that men may turn from me to glorify Thee.

6. Grant unto me, O God, I pray Thee, the indwelling of Thy Spirit, that I may have a right judgment in all things, and evermore rejoice in His Holy Comfort.

7. Thou, O God, art the Giver of all good and perfect gifts, and unto Thee I would render glory and praise; not only by my lips, but by giving myself up to Thy service and walking before Thee in holiness and righteousness all my days.

8. Help me to find my life according to Thy promise. I thank Thee that Thou hast implanted the germ of Thine own nature. Leave me not, neither forsake me in the toilsome, upward climb. Teach me to change my strength and mount up with the wings of eagles.

9. Let the Holy Ghost be to me a spirit of burning, consuming the dross and selfishness and suspicion of my heart, and kindling the pure flame of warm affection towards all who name the name of Christ in sincerity.

10. O Lord Jesus, hasten the time of the general homecoming, when we shall no longer be strangers and pilgrims, but enter in by the gates into the City, and meet again with our beloved, through the blood by which our garments are made whiter than snow.

11. Be not far from me, O Lord, this day; and through all its hours may I be found doing those things which are well pleasing in Thy sight; may I, like Enoch, walk with God, and, like him, have the testimony that I please God.

12. Almighty God, teach me the dignity of labor, the honor of industrious toil, the glory of being able to do something in the world. At the best I am an unprofitable servant: forgive, I pray Thee, my shortcomings and failure; prosper and establish the work of my hands.

13. Blessed be Thou, O Lord, for that Thou daily bearest my burdens, and loadest me with benefits. Thou art the God of my salvation; make my mountain to stand strong.

14. My Saviour, my heart is sorely broken as I think of all the sorrow and pain that I have given Thee. But let tears of gratitude mingle with those of penitential grief, as I remember Thy patient, abounding, unmerited love.

15. Father of Jesus, give me that same Holy Spirit, who raised Him from the dead, that He may raise me likewise. I long that His risen life may be more evidently mine; and that I may experience the power of His resurrection, rising as a fountain in my soul.

16. My Father, may the Holy Spirit enable me to realize in daily life my true position in Christ. Where He is, may I in heart and mind continually ascend and habitually dwell.

17. Grant me, O Lord, I beseech Thee, that through Thy grace the body of sin may be destroyed in me, and that through the power of Thy resurrection I may henceforth walk in newness of life.

18. Hasten, O God, to send Thy Holy Spirit upon the world in mighty power to convict men of sin and righteousness and judgment. May He work again as at Pentecost, that thousands may be stricken to the heart; and may times of refreshing come from Thy presence.

19. O Holy Saviour, make my life deeper, stronger, richer, gentler, more Christlike, more full of the spirit of heaven, more devoted to Thy service and glory. So that I may ever bless and praise Thee, and magnify Thy name and adorn Thy gospel in all things.

20. My Blessed Lord! Mercifully grant that I may both follow the example of Thy patience and be made a partaker of Thy kingdom, not only in the life which is to come, but here and now.

21. Most Holy God, I rejoice that the Saviour ever lives to intercede as our High Priest and Mediator. Through the rent veil let my prayers ascend to Thee, mingled with the fragrance of His perfect merit, in whom Thou art ever well pleased.

22. Dear Lord Jesus! I thank Thee that Thou lovest me, though most unworthy. I am the least of saints, and the chief of sinners, but in the bankruptcy of my soul I trust in the exceeding riches of Thy grace.

23. God of my fathers, I bless Thee that life is a pilgrimage; that the earth is not my rest; that every day brings me nearer my home in the City of God. I humbly thank Thee that Thou art willing to be my companion in every step of the desert march.

24. Most gracious God! Help me, I pray Thee, to exert a wholesome and gracious influence on those with whom I come into daily contact; diffusing in every look and gesture the sweet savor of Christ; and shedding in every act the genial light caught from His face.

25. Take my love, as the five barley loaves and two small fish and multiply it, that it may be sweet and refreshing to Thyself, and helpful to others.

26. Holy Saviour! I am often weary of myself, but do not Thou be weary of me; I am as the broken reed and the smouldering flax, but do not Thou be discouraged; leave me not comfortless, but come to me.

27. Enable me, O Lord, for Thy name's sake, to walk righteously and speak uprightly; to despise the gain of oppression and fraud; to keep my hands clean from unholy deeds; to stop my ears from uncharitable and polluting talk; to shut my eyes from beholding evil.

28. O God of Peace and Righteousness, may peace reign amid the nations of the earth, throughout our great industries, and between man and man. May war, slavery, impurity, blasphemy, and drunkenness, and all other evils which deprave and injure men, pass utterly away.

29. Heavenly Father! May I use aright the discipline through which I am passing, and learn to distinguish Thy meaning in every dark hour.

30. Great High Priest! I come to Thee with confession and faith. Deal not with me according to my sins, neither reward me according to mine iniquities. Teach me, through my penitence and sorrow, to hate evil more utterly, and by Thy grace to watch against it more carefully.

~~~~~ *October* ~~~~~

1. If my soul has turned perversely to the dark; if I have left some brother wounded by the way; if I have preferred my aims to Thine; if I have been impatient, and would not wait; if I have marred the pattern drawn out for my life; if I have cost tears to these I loved; if my heart has murmured against Thy will, O Lord forgive!

2. Enable me to do not only what I like to do, but what I ought. May I be guided, not by emotion, but by conscience. May I be content with the limits which Thy providence assigns. Cause me to be faithful in a little, and in common tasks to learn Thy deep lessons of patience, trust and conscientiousness.

3. Father, Thou hast loved us; Thou dost love us; Thou wilt love us forevermore. Thy love passes knowledge. It is like a warm, sunlit ocean enwrapping the tiny islet of my life. I bathe in it, but can never reach its limits. I thank Thee for its depths and lengths.

4. May I delight myself in Thee, Almighty God. Put gladness in my heart, more than in the time when corn and wine increase. Teach me how great is Thy goodness, and how great Thy beauty.

5. Give me grace to see the beauty lying at my feet in the commonplaces of life; and to feel that Thou art as near, and that life is as wonderful today, as when men beheld Thee in the days of Thy flesh.

6. Blessed Lord, may I find a balm for my own griefs, and a solace for my own disappointments, in sympathy and ministry to those whose hearts are breaking around me. Give me the quick eye and the skillful touch, that I may become like Barnabas, a son of consolation.

7. Lord Jesus, Thou hast revealed the Father, and hast brought us nigh unto God. I thank Thee that I may look unabashed upon the glory of the Eternal Throne, and know that all the attributes of Deity are now upon my side. Good and upright art Thou, Lord. I stand in Thee.

8. Blessed Christ! The storm is high and the night dark. Come to me, I beseech Thee.

9. May I dwell in Thee, O Christ, and Thou in me, that Thou mayest be magnified in my mortal body, whether by life or death. In the commonplaces of life may others see in me that which will remind them of Thee, my unseen Lord.

10. I beseech Thee, O Lord, to bless those whom I love. Minister to them as I would, could I be by their sides, and better than I could, because Thy thoughts and ways are so much more tender and helpful than mine could be. Keep them safe beneath Thy wing.

11. Take me to Thy heart, Heavenly Father. Kiss me, though stained with toil, travel and sin. Cover me with the seamless robe of our Saviour's righteousness. May I sit down at the table, and may Christ, the Door, intervene between me and the fret of the world.

12. Vouchsafe to keep me this day without sin. Into Thy hands I commit my spirit. Live in me, Blessed Lord, by Thy good Spirit, that my life may be an evangel of helpfulness and blessedness. Supply my daily needs. Teach me to exert a gracious and uplifting influence.

13. The world is dear to Thee, O Father. Thou didst send Thy Son to save it, send Thy Spirit to comfort and renew. May He brood over the chaos, as He did of old upon the deep. May order and peace reign among men; and may Jesus come quickly to receive His bride.

14. My Father, God! Enable me to roll my way upon Thee, to trust Thee, and to believe that when I stand with Thee in the perfect daylight I shall understand what now I take on trust. All Thy ways are mercy and truth.

15. For those I love, for all who are in sickness and sorrow, for those who anticipate this day with anxiety; for such as are called to suffer, to undergo special trial, to pass through the valley of the shadow, I humbly pray that they may be succored as they need.

16. Great, wonderful and gracious Father, I am tired with working, striving, thinking, and fall back upon Thy love, tenderer than a mother's and lasting as Thine own eternity. I cannot save this world, or carry its weight. Awake, awake, O Arm of the Lord.

17. O Divine Lord! When I am most absorbed in my necessary business, may Thy presence not withdraw itself, but be permanent and abiding. May I be faithful to Thee in little things, and be kept following the inner light, till it lead me into the perfect day.

18. Heavenly Father, I pray Thee to give us faith in Thy guardian care. May we realize that we are surrounded by hosts of watching angels. Bless and defend and save all whom we love, that they and we may be conscious partakers of Thy heavenly benediction.

19. I desire, O Lord, to take on me Thy yoke, and to learn Thy secret. Teach me to rejoice alway; to pray without ceasing; and in everything to give thanks.

20. I give thanks unto Thee with my whole heart, and sing praises unto Thy name for Thy loving-kindness and Thy truth. Bless the Lord, O my soul, and all that is within me bless His holy name! Hallelujah, for the Lord God Omnipotent reigneth!

21. I pray for my companions in life's pilgrimage; for the feeble and the ready-to-halt; for the despondent and the oppressed; for the poor and sick and forlorn. May their valleys of weeping become filled with springs of joy.

22. O Light of Life, shine upon my heart, that pines for the summer of Thy love. All Thy blessed saints, who gather around Thee in the world where night never comes, find in Thee their true consummation and bliss. Be to me what Thou art to them; and let me find in Thee the foretaste of heaven.

23. Undertake for the oppressed and weak, for women and children, for the slave and the prisoner. Watch by the bedside of the sleepless. Solace the heart of the bereaved. Hasten the coming of Thy kingdom, and the ingathering of Thine elect.

24. O Lord, who didst illumine the heart of Thomas with the clear radiance of Thy risen glory, Thou knowest how to deal with the doubts and perplexities of my heart. I have not seen; give me the blessedness of those who have believed.

25. Grant unto me "the hidden manna and the white stone." May I become a pillar in Thy temple, inscribed with Thine own new name. May I be clad in the white garment, have the anointed eye, and the gold refined by fire. Make me pure in Thy holiness, and more than a conqueror through Thy blood.

26. O Thou, who sat at Jacob's well, give me to drink of the river of the water of life, and to hear Thy voice, which is as music; and let that spring, of which Thou spakest, rise within my heart unto eternal life.

27. On this new day I adore Thee, my God and Father. The light is Thy garment; the heavens are the curtains of Thy home; the clouds Thy chariot; the winds Thy messengers; the fire Thy minister. Of Thee, and through Thee, and to Thee are all things. To Thee be glory.

28. Holy, Holy, Holy art Thou, O God! Heaven and earth are full of Thy glory. Every day is a day that Thou hast made. May I hunger no more, neither thirst any more, because I am abundantly satisfied with the fatness of Thy house, and have been made to drink of the river of Thy pleasures.

29. Thou covenant-keeping God! Thy faithfulness reacheth unto the skies—help me to reckon upon it in every step of this day's pilgrimage. Thy righteousness is like the great mountains—may I keep in view of it always.

30. My Master and Lord! May I know that Thou goest before, as of old, before Thy disciples. The sword pierces Thy heart before it touches mine, and the waves spend themselves on Thee before I am wetted by their spray. The heavy part of my cross rests on Thee.

31. Make me to hate evil, and to cleave to that which is good. Take from me the heart of stone, and give me the heart of flesh. Deliver me from my idols. Take from me the love of sin. Put Thy Spirit within me, and cause me to walk in Thy way.

November

1. Gracious Lord, forgive the past. Keep me as the apple of Thine eye. Encompass me with Thy guardian care, and realize in me Thy highest purposes. So will I offer in Thy tabernacles sacrifices of joy. I will sing, yea, I will sing praises unto the Lord.

2. I adore Thee, Holy Father! There is no limit to Thy power, or to Thy love. Thou art greatly to be praised! Thou art greatly to be loved! There is none like unto Thee, glorious in holiness, fearful in praises, doing wonders. Accept the homage of my soul and life, through Jesus Christ.

3. O God! Make me increasingly conscious, I beseech Thee, of the indwelling of Thy Holy Spirit; may He witness with my spirit that in spite of all my sin I am still Thy child; may He enable me to reckon myself dead to the solicitations of the Tempter.

4. Accept what I have done for Thy Church and glory, great Lord. Though it be little in the eye of man, may it be much to Thee. Teach me to remember that I am made a priest, and to realize that every sphere may be a temple for service and each act a sacrament.

5. May Thy Word be increasingly precious to me, O Lord; and in Thy words may I ever hear the Word. Beholding Thy face in this mirror, may I become changed.

6. There are so many mysteries in the world, and in human life, O Lord. My eyes are tired of straining into the dark. I can only follow on to know Thee, but I believe that Thy going forth is prepared as the morning. In the meanwhile refresh my heart as the rain.

7. Thine, O Lord, is the greatness and the power, and the glory, and the victory, and the majesty; for all that is in the heaven and in the earth is Thine. Thine is the kingdom, O Lord, and Thou art exalted Head above all. Glory be to Thee!

8. Gracious, Holy Savior! Cleanse my tears, purify my penitence, refine my hope, and accept me as needy and helpless, who can claim nothing; but I count on Thee because Thou hast bidden all who are weary and heavy-laden to come.

9. Holy Saviour! Undertake the care of our failures that might lead us to despond, and the joy of our successes that might induce pride. Make right what is wrong; undo what is done amiss; stablish, strengthen and prosper all Thou canst use.

10. Lord Jesus! Teach me how to apply to the common things of daily life the heavenly principles of the Risen life. May I esteem nothing common or unclean. May every common bush be aflame with God.

11. Vouchsafe to keep me, O Lord, this day free from known sin. May I fall into no sin, neither run into any kind of danger, but may all my doings be ordered by Thy governance, to do always that which is pleasing in Thy sight.

12. Heavenly Father! Deal not with me after my sins, negligences, and ignorances. Cleanse my fouled soul and defiled garments. Forsake not the work of Thine own hands. Perfect that which concerneth me, because Thy mercy endureth forever.

13. Heavenly Father! Put all my sins behind Thee into the depths of the sea. Deliver me from the dominion and love of sin. Cause all grace to abound towards me, that I may have all sufficiency for all things, and abound to every good work.

14. Eternal God! As my outward man decays, may the inward man be renewed day by day, and may my light affliction, which is but for a moment, work out for me a far more exceeding and eternal weight of glory.

15. Lord Jesus! I pray for Thy one Church, the members of which are scattered in many different sects and over the wide world. They who are one with Thee must be one with each other; but grant that our unity may stand revealed and confessed, so that men may believe.

16. The good I would, I do not; the evil that I would not, I do. Alas, for my temper, my pride, my self-will, the bad thoughts I permit, the unkind, rash things I say! But Thou knewest all before Thou didst awaken me. Pity and save me!

17. Take me as I return home to Thee, soiled and dusty with the sin and business of the day. Cleanse me from all unrighteousness, not only with the grace of forgiveness, but with the grace that passes through every chamber of the inner life, purifying and sanctifying all.

18. Heavenly Father! I thank Thee for the gift of Thy Son, who is the Pearl of Great Price; the Hidden Treasure, which makes the soul rich for ever; the Delight of Heaven; the Glory of His Church; the All-sufficient Portion of His Own.

19. Heavenly Father! Hasten in all lands the reign of Thy Son; may all kings fall down before Him, all nations serve Him. Let His name endure forever, and be continued as long as the sun, and all mankind be blessed in Him.

20. Teach me, O Lord, the way of Thy statutes, and I shall keep them unto the end. Give me understanding that I may keep Thy law. Make me to keep the path of Thy commandments, for therein do I delight.

21. If it is Thy will that temptation should come upon me today, may I not distrust Thy leading hand, nor think that failure is inevitable, nor concern myself too much with our great adversary. Be with me when I am surrounded by the wild beasts, and let angels minister.

22. Hear my prayer for our country, for those who exercise authority, or enact laws, or pronounce judicial decisions. Enlighten those who teach the young, or write books, or edit newspapers. Give peace in our time, good Lord, I beseech Thee.

23. Forgiving Saviour! If I have in my heart aught against my brother, may I have the grace of silence concerning it to others and the grace of speech about it to him alone. Let the love that covereth a multitude of sins be mine.

24. Holy Father! I mourn the divisions which divide Thy people, and humbly entreat Thee to fulfill the prayer of our Blessed Lord, that the people whom He purchased for a possession "may all be one," even as Thou, Father, art in Him and He in Thee.

25. Blessed is the man whose strength is in Thee, my God, and in whose heart are Thy ways. May that strength be mine, yet not mine, but Thine perfected in my weakness. May my heart be strong to hope, to love, and to endure.

26. O strong Son of God, Who art like the sun going forth from his chamber, and rejoicing as a strong man to run his race, gather me up into fellowship with Thee in Thy strength and pity, and in Thy tenderness towards the weary and weak.

27. To Thee, Heavenly Father, I commend my comrades and friends, on every part of life's great battlefield. Let no defeat discourage them. Let no sudden temptation overcome them. Let no long-continued sorrow wear out their loyalty, or discourage their faith.

28. O Blessed Master, draw me aside into sympathy with Thyself, in Thy ceaseless intercessions for Thy Church and for the world. Let it not be enough for Thee to pray for me; oh, pray in me. Let Thy prayers pass up through my lips.

29. O Thou that hearest prayer! Let the voice of supplication be always audible in the Holy of Holies of my spirit. May I pray with the faith to which Thou canst entrust the key of Thy treasury.

30. Though my outward life be a desert march, may my heart live in the heavenly places, whither the Forerunner has entered. May I eat of the fruit of the land, and drink of the River of God, and have unbroken victory over all that opposes.

~ December ~

1. My Saviour and Exemplar! I pray for others; for those who misunderstand and injure me; for any I have wronged; for those to whom in past days I may have been a stumbling block; for such as might have been saved if I had been more faithful. Do for them by other means what I might have done.

2. Forbid, O Heavenly Father, that I should ever lose the freshness, fertility, and beauty which Thou canst maintain in hearts which are open to Thee. May it be my lot today, amid the pressing duties of daily toil, to have a fresh, holy, and fragrant spirit.

3. For all Thy gracious care I reverently thank Thee; and if Thou hast permitted things to happen which have tried me sore, and filled me with bitterness, help me to trust in Thine infinite love, that through the discipline I may be weaned from all that grieves Thee.

4. O Saviour! Forgive my sins, my faithless tears, and my repining murmurs; my thoughtlessness of others and my self-centered anxiety. Lift me on to the tide of Thy love, and up to fuller, richer, deeper levels of experience.

5. Great Shepherd! Lead me amid the pastures of tender grass, and by the waters of rest; or if my way lie amid rocks and desert places, prevent me with blessings of goodness, and let Thy rod and staff be my comfort.

6. Hasten Thy coming Lord Jesus, to right the wrongs of time, and establish Thine everlasting kingdom. Grant unto me, though most unworthy, to sit with Thee at Thy table, and see Thee, when Thou art crowned in the joy of Thine espousals.

7. How great is Thy goodness, great God, which Thou hast laid up for them that fear Thee, which Thou hast wrought for them that trust in Thee before the sons of men! Of Thee, and through Thee, and to Thee are all things, and to Thee shall be the glory forever.

8. Lord Jesus! Make the fountain of my heart purer, that the streams may be purer also. May my heart indite good matter, that my mouth may speak of our King. May my conversation be with grace, seasoned with salt, full of truth and love and strength.

9. Thou makest Thine abode, O God, with those who are of a humble and contrite spirit, and who tremble at Thy Word. Take my weakness up into Thy strength; my ignorance into Thy wisdom; my changefulness into Thine everlasting constancy.

10. Gracious Father, I thank Thee for the Son of Thy love, for all that He has done for us, and will do; for all that He has been to us, and will be. I thank thee that He holds me in His strong, pierced hand, and loves me with the love that cannot let me go.

11. My Father! Teach me to trust Thy love. May I dare to believe it when the dark clouds brood, as well as when the sun shines. May I never doubt that Thou art doing Thy best for me, and that what I know not now, I shall know hereafter.

12. Great Maker of Men! I am nothing better than common earthenware; but may I be cleansed and purified, and filled with Thy heavenly treasure. Dip me deep into the river of life, and give refreshment through me to many parched and weary hearts.

13. Great Lord of all! I pray for this great world, especially for those who in distant lands are going forth bearing the precious need. Bless them in their work, and encourage them when their hearts are faint. May they remember that they are fellow workers with Thee.

14. Holy Spirit! May my heart be filled with Thy love, my lips with gentle, helpful words, and my hands with kind, unselfish deeds. May those who see me take knowledge of me that I have been with Jesus. May the fragrance of His presence be shed abroad in every act.

15. I humbly ask, O Christ, that Thy peace may be the garrison of my heart, with its affections, and of my mind with its many thoughts; that it may ever rule within me, asserting itself over the tumultuous passions that rise within. And out of this peace may I arise to serve.

16. Giver of Peace! May peace be within this house; peace be in the homes of those that love me; peace be with all tired workers, and lonely pilgrims, and sin-weary hearts; peace be with Thy Church, that her schism and discord may be ended, Thy peace, Heavenly Father!

17. Thou hast taught me to look for the time when the creation shall be made free with the glorious liberty of the sons of God. Hasten that glorious day, O Lord, when Thine own hand shall wipe tears from off all faces, and the former things shall have passed away.

18. Gracious Lord! May the Holy Spirit keep me ever walking in the light of Thy countenance. May He fill my heart with the sense of Thy nearness and loving fellowship. Order my steps in Thy way, and then walk with me. Teach me to do the thing that pleaseth Thee.

19. Father! My heart misgives me somewhat as I contrast the spirit of Thy Blessed Son with the storm and strife of life; but Thou be with me; and may my soul keep its Sabbaths.

20. Great Burden-bearer, I bring to Thee my anxieties and cares; about myself and my dear ones; about my body and soul; about the things of this life and those of eternity. I cannot carry them; they rob me of peace and strength. Wilt Thou take them, Heavenly Lord, and carry them for me.

21. Great Saviour, who didst send the Comforter! For the temptations which He has overcome in us; for the comfort He has given us; for the fruits He has wrought in us; for the glimpses of Thy love He has unfolded; and for the hopes He has inspired, I lovingly thank Thee.

22. Great God! Teach me the art of so living in fellowship with Thee that every act may be a psalm, every meal a sacrament, every room a sanctuary, and every thought a prayer. May the bells that ring to common duty be inscribed with "Holiness to the Lord."

23. Most blessed Lord, may all uncleanness and filthiness, foolish talking, and covetousness, bitterness, wrath and anger be put away from me, with all malice. May I forgive even as God in Christ has forgiven me.

24. Hasten the coming of Thy kingdom and to this end further with Thy ready help every true worker for Thee, the world over. May the kingdoms of this world speedily become the kingdoms of our God, and of His Christ. Help me to speed the coming of that day.

CHRISTMAS DAY

25. O Thou who didst send forth Thy Son! May the purity, simplicity, and beauty of the Holy Child, Jesus, be poured like a sweet fragrance through our hearts and lives. Bless the absent and those we love, the strangers and the lonely, and may we all meet in the great home-coming.

26. O Saviour, I commend to Thee those whom I have injured, or spoken against, or failed to help. I pray for those who have treated me wrongfully and despitefully. I intercede for my dear ones, for all sufferers and mourners, and for Thy saints everywhere.

27. Blessed Lord, may I be strong, not for myself alone, but for others. Teach me to bear the infirmities of the weak, to succor those that are overborne in the fight of life, and to lighten the load of care beneath which many of my fellow believers are pressed to the earth.

28. Holy Spirit, make me merciful in my judgment of others. May I think no evil. Deliver me from the spirit of retaliation. Help me to speak and think of others as I would have them do of myself. O, make me pure in heart; not only in my outward walk, but in my inward temper.

29. May I be kept, O Gracious Master, from the corruption which is in the world through lust. May my speech be always with grace, seasoned with salt. May my behavior be as becoming the gospel of Christ. May there be nothing in my loneliest moments to keep me from Thee.

30. O Head of the Church, I would intercede on the behalf of all who minister in Thy Holy Gospel. Enrich them with knowledge and utterance. As they break the living Bread, may they be nourished. As the river flows through them to others, may it keep their hearts fresh and fruitful.

The Last Day of the Year

31. Through the year Thou has brought me, O gracious God, to this hour. Accept my deep and loving thanks. I trust Thee for what Thou hast withheld, as I bless Thee for what Thou hast given. May goodness and mercy bring me to the many mansions; and be Thou near me through all the days unto the end.